FEELINGS
1 Joy

Tamra B. Orr

CHERRY
LAKE
Publishing

Published in the United States of America
by Cherry Lake Publishing
Ann Arbor, Michigan
www.cherrylakepublishing.com

Reading Adviser: Marla Conn MS, Ed., Literacy specialist, Read-Ability, Inc.

Photo Credits: © Andy Dean Photography/Shutterstock Images, cover, 1; © Samuel Borges Photography/Shutterstock Images, 4; © mimagephotography/Shutterstock Images, 6; © warrengoldswain/Shutterstock Images, 8; © Golden Pixels LLC/Shutterstock Images, 10; © Rob Hainer/Shutterstock Images, 12; © Andresr/Shutterstock Images, 14; © Dragon Images/Shutterstock Images, 16; © Ronnachai Palas/Shutterstock Images, 18; © frechtoch/Shutterstock Images, 20

Library of Congress Cataloging-in-Publication Data

Names: Orr, Tamra, author.
Title: Joy / Tamra B. Orr.
Description: Ann Arbor : Cherry Lake Publishing, 2016. | Series: Feelings | Audience: K to Grade 3. | Includes bibliographical references and index.
Identifiers: LCCN 2015048111| ISBN 9781634710442 (hardcover) | ISBN 9781634711432 (pdf) | ISBN 9781634712422 (pbk.) | ISBN 9781634713412 (ebook)
Subjects: LCSH: Joy--Juvenile literature.
Classification: LCC BF575.H27 O77 2016 | DDC 152.4/2--dc23
LC record available at https://lccn.loc.gov/2015048111

Cherry Lake Publishing would like to acknowledge the work of The Partnership for 21st Century Learning. Please visit www.p21.org for more information.

Printed in the United States of America
Corporate Graphics

Table of Contents

How can you tell this girl is joyful?

Joy

I smile when I feel joyful.
See my teeth?

I laugh when I feel *really* joyful.

I feel warm inside and out.

How are this mom and daughter feeling?

8

Family and Friends

My family makes me joyful. They hug me!

My friends make me joyful.
We talk and play.

My dog makes me joyful. He licks my face!

Playing Outside

Sunshine makes me joyful.

I run and play at **recess**.

Why are these girls joyful?

I smile on the swing.

I laugh **slipping** down the slide.

Joyful Dreams

I am joyful when I curl up in bed.

I pull the **covers** up. It is time to **dream**.

Joyful dreams make me smile, too.

Find Out More

Adler, Esther. *Happy: Helping Children Embrace Happiness.* New York: Bright Awareness Publications, 2014.

Hahn, Daniel, and Stella Dreis. *Happiness Is a Watermelon on Your Head*. London: Phoenix Yard Books, 2012.

Glossary

covers (KUHV-urz) blankets
dream (DREEM) to imagine events while you are sleeping
recess (REE-ses) a break in the school day
slipping (SLIP-ing) to move quickly and smoothly

Home and School Connection

Use this list of words from the book to help your child become a better reader. Word games and writing activities can help beginning readers reinforce literacy skills.

and	inside	slide
bed	joyful	slipping
covers	laugh	smile
curl	licks	sunshine
dog	make	swing
down	makes	talk
dream	out	teeth
dreams	play	the
face	pull	they
family	really	time
feel	recess	too
friends	run	warm
hug	see	when

Index

About the Author

Tamra Orr has written more than 400 books for young people. The only thing she loves more than writing books is reading them. She lives in beautiful Portland, Oregon, with her husband, four children, dog, and cat. Each one of them makes her very happy every day.